976.1
PEZ

Pezzi, Bryan
Arkansas
34880000 822945

ARKANSAS

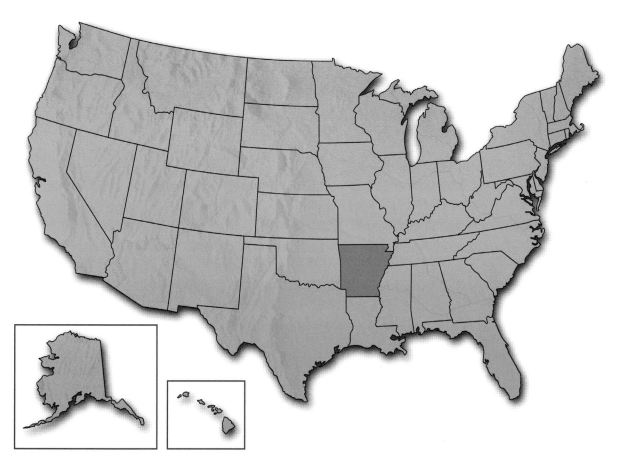

Bryan Pezzi

Published by Weigl Publishers Inc.
123 South Broad Street, Box 227
Mankato, MN   56002
USA
Web site: http://www.weigl.com

Library of Congress Cataloging-in-Publication Data available upon request from the publisher. Fax: (507)388-2746 for the attention of the Publishing Records Department.

ISBN 1-930954-82-4 (lib. bdg.)
ISBN 1-930954-73-5 (pbk.)

Printed in the United States of America
1 2 3 4 5 6 7 8 9 0   05 04 03 02 01

Project Coordinator
Jennifer Nault
Substantive Editor
Rennay Craats
Copy Editor
Heather Kissock
Designers
Warren Clark
Terry Paulhus
Photo Researcher
Angela Lowen

Photograph Credits

Every reasonable effort has been made to trace ownership and to obtain permission to reprint copyright material. The publishers would be pleased to have any errors or omissions brought to their attention so that they may be corrected in subsequent printings.

Cover: Father and Son Hiking (Photodisc Corporation), Diamonds (BHP Diamonds Inc.) **Archive Photos:** pages 19BL, 21T, 23T, 23BL, 24T, 27ML; **Arkansas History Commission:** pages 3M, 17T, 17BR, 18T, 18BR, 19T, 19BR; **Arkansas Parks and Tourism:** pages 3B, 4T, 4ML, 4BR, 5T, 6T, 7T, 8T, 8BL, 8BR, 9T, 9B, 10BL, 11BR, 12T, 12ML, 12BR, 13T, 13BR, 14BR, 16T, 16B, 17BL, 18BL, 20T, 20BL, 20BR, 21B, 22T, 22ML, 22BR, 23BR, 24ML, 25BR, 26T, 26 BL, 26BR, 27TR, 27B, 28T, 29T, 29B; **Corel Corporation:** pages 3T, 10T, 10BR, 11T, 11ML, 13BL, 15ML, 25BL; **Defense Visual Information Center:** page 14T; **Eyewire Corporation:** pages 14BL, 28B; **Hot Springs Visitor's Bureau:** page 6BR; **Little Rock Convention and Visitor's Bureau:** page 7B; **Photodisc:** page 6BL; **Photofest:** pages 24BR, 25T, **Monique de St. Croix:** pages 15T, 15BR.

CONTENTS

Lake Ouachita is the largest lake in the state of Arkansas.

INTRODUCTION

Arkansas is known for its southern charm and natural wonders. Officially recognized as "The Natural State," Arkansas has rugged mountains, clear lakes and streams, and an abundance of natural wildlife. The southwest is known for its oil fields and grazing cattle, and the northwest is characterized by dairy farms and orchards. In the east, near the Mississippi River, cotton **plantations** are much like those of the Deep South. Over the past 500 years, Arkansas has developed from a vast, unoccupied wilderness to a modern, progressive state. Its industries include agriculture, technology, and commerce. Arkansas has a wealth of natural resources, but the friendly people are the state's greatest asset.

QUICK FACTS

Magazine Mountain is the state's highest point at 2,753 feet above sea level.

The forty-carat "Uncle Sam" diamond is the largest diamond ever found in the United States. It was unearthed in 1924 in Murfreesboro.

At 53,182 square miles, Arkansas is the twenty-eighth largest state.

Arkansas entered the Union on June 15, 1836. It was the twenty-fifth state to join.

Many horseback riders are drawn to the Ouachita Mountains to explore the stunning beauty of the area.

The state of Arkansas has nearly 3,000 miles of railroad track.

Getting There

Arkansas is located in the western portion of the south-central portion of the United States. It is bordered by six other states. In the east, the Mississippi River separates Arkansas from both Tennessee and Mississippi. Missouri lies to the north of Arkansas, and Louisiana lies to the south. Arkansas is bordered by Texas and Oklahoma to the west.

Visitors can travel to Arkansas by car, bus, plane, or train. Major transportation routes pass through Little Rock, the state capital. Interstates 40 and 30 lead to Little Rock, as do US Highways 65 and 67. Most major airlines touch down and take off at Little Rock National Airport, which is located 5 miles east of Little Rock.

QUICK FACTS

Arkansas's state motto is *Regnat Populus*. This Latin phrase, adopted in 1907, means "The People Rule."

In 1861, Arkansas and ten other southern states attempted to form an independent country called the Confederate States of America.

Arkansas was originally part of the Louisiana Purchase of 1803. In this deal, the United States paid France $15 million for 828,000 square miles of land.

Since the 1830s, the area that is now known as Hot Springs National Park has provided soothing waters to many well-known figures, including Franklin D. Roosevelt, Babe Ruth, and Al Capone.

Arkansas Location Map

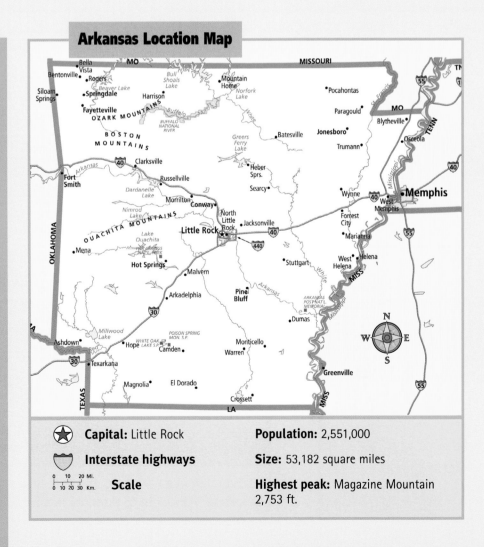

⭐ **Capital:** Little Rock

🛡 **Interstate highways**

Scale 0 10 20 Mi. / 0 10 20 30 Km.

Population: 2,551,000

Size: 53,182 square miles

Highest peak: Magazine Mountain 2,753 ft.

Arkansas's Ouachita National Forest covers 1.6 million acres of land.

QUICK FACTS

Arkansas has been called "The Bowie State" after a famous knife that was made for Colonel James Bowie. A Bowie knife is a sharp, pointed, hunting knife.

Ouachita National Forest is the oldest and largest national forest in the South.

Pine Bluff is known as one of the world's largest producers of archery bows.

The name "Arkansas" reflects the early influence of Native-American and French cultures in the area. When French explorers discovered a group of Native Peoples called Arkansea, they modified the word slightly to "Arkansas." *Arkansea* means "the people who live downstream." For many years, residents disagreed about how the word should be pronounced. Some people said AR-kan-SAW, while others insisted it was Ar-KANSAS. In 1881, the state's General Assembly decided that the name would be spelled "Arkansas," but pronounced "Arkansaw."

In addition to the "The Natural State," Arkansas has gained many other nicknames throughout its history. As early as 1875, the state was billed as "The Land of Opportunity" in an effort to attract new residents. Some people call Arkansas "The Hot Water State" for its many hot springs.

Bathing in, or even drinking, the pure water from Arkansas's many hot springs is thought to promote healing and relaxation.

Like every state, Arkansas has special state symbols. The state flag was designed in 1913 by Willie K. Hocker, a woman from Wabbaseka. It has twenty-five white stars on a blue border, signifying Arkansas's status as the twenty-fifth state to join the Union. There are also four blue stars around the word "Arkansas." These stars represent the four nations that have governed Arkansas: France, Spain, the Confederate States of America, and the United States of America. A white diamond represents Arkansas's status as the most important diamond-producing state in the Union.

The state seal was adopted in 1864. It bears the words "Great Seal of Arkansas." On the seal is a bald eagle surrounded by three figures—the Angel of Mercy, the Goddess of Liberty, and the Sword of Justice. Below these figures, a shield features a steamboat, plow, beehive, and a sheaf of wheat. These symbols represent the state's early industries.

QUICK FACTS

Arkansas has a salute to the state flag: "I Salute the Arkansas Flag With Its Diamond and Stars. We Pledge Our Loyalty to Thee."

The oldest part of Little Rock is known as the Quapaw Quarter. It has many fine examples of Victorian architecture.

Arkansas experienced an incredible population boom between 1810 and 1820. Nearly 49,000 new settlers arrived in the region during that time.

The state's waters drain southeastward, toward the Mississippi River.

The population of Arkansas is more than 2.5 million.

The Ozark Mountains rise to 2,000 feet above sea level.

Arkansas's rivers include the Mississippi, Arkansas, Ouachita, Red, White, and St. Francis.

Arkansas has many reservoirs, which were formed by damming natural waterways.

Lake Chicot is the state's largest natural lake.

There are more than 9,000 miles of streams and rivers in Arkansas.

LAND AND CLIMATE

On a map, a diagonal line drawn from St. Francis to Texarkana will divide Arkansas into two triangular segments. The lowlands are in the southeast, and the highlands are in the northwest. The southeastern part of the state, which features low, level plains, has the best farming land in the state. The northwestern highlands are composed of mountains and deep valleys.

Arkansas has two main mountain ranges. The Ozark Mountains in the north are home to dense forests and gurgling rivers and brooks. In western and central Arkansas are the Ouachita Mountains. This area is rich in coal and natural gas. The Arkansas Valley lies between the Ozark and the Ouachita Mountains.

Arkansas's climate is warm and wet. Summers are long and hot, with temperatures occasionally rising above 100° Fahrenheit. Typically, July temperatures soar to about 80°F. Winters are short and mild. January temperatures average between 38°F and 46°F. Arkansas has an average rainfall of 50 inches per year and an average snowfall of 6 inches per year.

People can see some interesting rock formations and waterfalls while hiking in the Natural State.

NATURAL RESOURCES

Arkansas has one of only two diamond mines in the United States—the other is in Colorado.

Nature has blessed Arkansas with many resources. The state is the only one in the nation that produces diamonds on a continuous basis. Diamond mining began in 1906, when John Huddleston spotted two of the glittering stones in his southwest Arkansas field. His land became the only diamond mine in the country at the time. Today, visitors can search for diamonds at Crater of Diamonds State Park in Murfreesboro. They can even keep any diamonds they find while digging! More than 70,000 diamonds have been found in the Crater of Diamonds State Park.

Quartz crystal is another important mineral found in Arkansas. These crystals are sometimes called "Arkansas diamonds," but they are not true diamonds. Quartz crystals are mined in the Ouachita Mountains and are used in computer components. This stone became Arkansas's state mineral in 1967.

Crater of Diamonds State Park is the only public diamond mine in the world.

UNCLE SAM DIAMOND

PLANTS AND ANIMALS

The Natural State lives up to its nickname. Over half of Arkansas is wooded. Forests and natural areas provide habitats for many plant and animal species.

Opossums, muskrats, weasels, rabbits, and squirrels can all be found in Arkansas. Red and gray foxes also roam throughout the state. Government game **refuges** maintain deer and elk populations in Arkansas.

There are many forested areas in Arkansas's mountain highlands. Hardwood forests of oak, hickory, maple, and beech stretch across the Ozark Mountains. In the Ouachita Mountains, shortleaf pine forests thrive. There are rare fish in the upland streams and salamanders on the moist mountain slopes. The highland regions are also home to black bears and bobcats.

The bobcat, a close relative of the lynx, roams the state of Arkansas.

QUICK FACTS

The apple blossom is Arkansas's state flower. It has pink and white petals. At one time, Arkansas was a major apple-producing state.

Arkansas's state bird is the mockingbird. This bird mocks, or imitates, the songs of many other birds.

The pine is the state tree. Two varieties, the loblolly and the shortleaf, are found in the state. Both varieties may grow to be 100 feet tall.

In southern Arkansas, pine forests prevail. White-tailed deer and the **endangered** red-cockaded woodpecker live in this area. This particular type of woodpecker is very rare and lives only in old-growth pine forests.

Arkansas's eastern border is part of the Mississippi Delta region. Swamps and **bayous** support cypress trees and water tupelo. The state's wetlands are also an important winter haven for migrating birds. White River National Wildlife Refuge provides a winter home for Canada geese and mallard ducks. Some of the birds rest and feed in the fields before flying farther south toward the Gulf of Mexico.

Many varieties of brightly-colored and sweet-smelling flowers bloom in most parts of the state. Passionflowers, water lilies, and thirty-six different kinds of orchids grow in Arkansas. There are many different kinds of wildflowers found in forested areas, including the American bellflower, aster, verbena, phlox, and wild hydrangea.

The white-tailed deer is the state mammal of Arkansas—along with ten other states.

QUICK FACTS

The honeybee is Arkansas's state insect. A picture of a dome beehive can be found on the Great Seal of Arkansas.

There are 130 varieties of fish in Arkansas's lakes and streams. The most common are catfish, bream, crappie, and bass.

The white-tailed deer is Arkansas's state mammal. This variety of deer raises the white underside of its tail when frightened.

The scarlet tanager is a small bird found throughout the Arkansas highlands. The male is known for its bright red feathers.

Many tourists are drawn to the Natural State to experience its varied beauty.

TOURISM

Whether people come to the state to enjoy the great outdoors or to learn about United States history, visitors to Arkansas will not be disappointed. There is much to see and do. The Natural State's many attractions draw 15 million tourists and bring in about $2 billion each year.

The state capital, Little Rock, is a good place to begin a tour of Arkansas. Little Rock has many historic sites for visitors to enjoy. The Old State House was home to Arkansas's government from 1836 to 1911. Today, the building, constructed of handmade brick, is a historical museum.

Beyond Little Rock, tourists flock to the mountains to enjoy hiking, camping, and fishing. The Ozark and Ouachita Mountains are especially popular for their beautiful scenery. Arkansas is also home to many natural hot springs. Bubbling hot springs can be found in the towns of Eureka Springs, Hot Springs, and Mammoth Springs. After a day of sight-seeing, people can soak their travel-weary muscles in these soothing waters.

Visitors to Arkansas can see the Old State House Museum, which is the original Arkansas State House.

Watermelons, one of Arkansas's many fruit crops, are originally from tropical Africa.

INDUSTRY

Agriculture has always been an important industry in Arkansas. Watermelons, grapes, blueberries, and apples are all grown in the state. Of all the crops that grow in Arkansas, rice is the most important. Arkansas produces more rice than any other state.

In the plains of eastern Arkansas, farmers grow rice in flat fields. Young rice plants must be kept wet. Farmers build earth banks around their fields and then pump in enough water to cover the plants. The rice plants are submerged under 2 to 6 inches of water until the grain starts to ripen. Then the water is drained, and the rice is harvested.

Chickens are another valuable farm product. In fact, Arkansas leads all other states in poultry production. The state raises about 1 billion chickens each year. Most are raised for their meat, and others for their eggs. Every year, Arkansas chickens produce about 4 billion eggs.

In addition to agriculture, Arkansas also has a large manufacturing industry. Electrical equipment, paper products, wood products, chemicals, and machinery are all produced in the state.

Crop dusters fly low to the ground. This helps prevent the chemicals that are released from drifting to other crops.

Little Rock Air Force Base trains many government military workers.

The state government provides a great motivation for companies to move to Arkansas—it has the second lowest tax burden of any state in the nation.

Arkansas has a number of leather and textile plants.

With more than 1,150 employees, the Maybelline cosmetic company provides jobs to many people living in Pulaski County.

GOODS AND SERVICES

Many Arkansans make a living providing goods and services. For example, some people provide educational services. These people are teachers, principals, and college instructors. Arkansas has more than 1,000 public schools and more than 200 private schools. There are also thirty colleges and twenty-three **vocational** schools. Hospitality and tourism workers provide services, too. They work in restaurants, hotels, and tourist information centers.

Government workers make up about 14 percent of the state's total work force. Not all government employees work in office buildings—some work in any of Arkansas's three national forests and forty-eight state parks. These people include rangers, wardens, and interpreters. Other government workers include military soldiers and civil servants. Many work in the state capital, Little Rock.

Resource Raccoon is the official mascot of Arkansas's state parks.

The Jacuzzi brothers from Arkansas invented and marketed the world's first whirlpool bath in 1968.

Berryville is known as the "Turkey Capital of Arkansas." The town raises more than 500,000 turkeys each year.

Fayetteville's Arkansas Industrial University opened in 1871. It later became the University of Arkansas.

The state has about 143 newspapers, 29 of which are dailies.

The South Arkansas vine ripe pink tomato is the official state fruit. It was chosen in 1987.

About 1.2 million people are employed in the state. The largest number of people, 24 percent, work in the service sector. About 21 percent are employed in the wholesale or retail trades, and 18 percent are employed in manufacturing. Others work in government, transportation, finance, and agriculture.

In the past, Arkansas's economy relied on agricultural goods. Today, many more companies are doing business in the state. Arkansas is a home office state for large companies that include Jacuzzi, Tyson Foods, Riceland Foods, Maybelline, Dillards Department Store, and J. B. Hunt Transport Company. Based in Little Rock, Stephens Incorporated is the largest investment firm in the country, besides those found on Wall Street.

One of the most famous goods providers in the United States originated in Arkansas. The Wal-Mart chain of stores sells a variety of items, from clothing, to toys, to household appliances. The company was founded by Sam Walton, who lived from 1918 to 1992. The first Wal-Mart opened in Rogers, Arkansas, in 1962. By 1992, Wal-Mart had become the largest retail chain in the world.

Wal-Mart has expanded since its early days. There are now stores in all fifty states.

Many of the artifacts that have been found in Arkansas help archeologists learn about the state's early peoples.

FIRST NATIONS

Archeologists believe people have lived in the Arkansas area for at least 12,000 years. These early cultures left behind mounds, stone objects, and pottery. Arkansas's early inhabitants are the ancestors of many of today's Native Americans. Arkansas offered fertile soil and an abundance of wildlife. The first Native Peoples in the area were hunter-gatherers who lived in caves. Over the centuries, these groups developed into farming communities that lived in permanent villages. Early Native Peoples included the Folsom, Bluff Dwellers, Mound Builders, Choctaw, and Cherokee.

At the time of European settlement, there were three main groups of Native Peoples in the area. The Osage were hunters in northern Arkansas, and the Caddo lived along the Red River in the southern part of the state. The Quapaw built villages at the mouth of the Arkansas River. Many Native Peoples in Arkansas grew pumpkins and corn and hunted wild animals. During the early nineteenth century, they had to give up much of their land to settlers. From 1820 to 1840, the government forced Native Peoples to leave Arkansas and other southeastern states. Many Native Americans **relocated** to Oklahoma.

The Toltec Mounds were built between 600 and 950 AD.

QUICK FACTS

The Bluff Dwellers lived in caves along the White River. They made their homes under rock shelves.

Early Native Peoples built dirt mounds near riverbanks. Some were used as burial places. Others were places of safety during floods.

Arkansas's tallest dirt mounds are the Toltec Mounds near Little Rock. The largest of these mounds is 50 feet high.

From 1838 to 1839, the Cherokee were made to travel across northern Arkansas on their way to government-designated land. This route has become known as the "Trail of Tears."

The Arkansas Post was established by Henri de Tonti. The post drew many people to the interior of North America.

In 1800, there were only about 400 people of European heritage in the state of Arkansas.

A huge logjam called the "Great Raft" made navigation on the Red River difficult until 1838.

Arkansas was ruled first by France, then by Spain, and then again by France before it was sold to the United States in 1803.

Today, people can visit the Arkansas Post National Memorial on the site of Henri de Tonti's original settlement.

EXPLORERS AND MISSIONARIES

The Spanish explorer Hernando de Soto was the first European to come to Arkansas. He arrived in 1541 during an unsuccessful **expedition** for gold. Two Frenchmen, Louis Joliet and Father Jacques Marquette, visited the area 132 years later. They canoed down the Mississippi River and reached the Arkansas River in 1673. Marquette was a missionary who wanted to teach Christianity to the Native Peoples, and Joliet was a fur trader.

In 1682, French explorer René-Robert Cavelier, also known as Sieur de La Salle, arrived at the mouth of the Mississippi River. He claimed all of the Mississippi Valley for France. Cavelier called this region Louisiana in honor of the King of France, Louis XIV. Arkansas was included in this territory.

Cavelier's lieutenant, Henri de Tonti, established the Arkansas Post in 1686. This fur-trading post was the first European settlement in Arkansas. That is why Tonti is known as the "Father of Arkansas."

When Hernando de Soto came to Arkansas, he brought along 100 horses and an army of more than 500 men.

In Arkansas's early days, most movement to and from the state was made in river flatboats.

EARLY SETTLERS

The first large group of European settlers came to Arkansas in 1717. At this time, several hundred Germans and Dutch arrived at Arkansas Post. However, by 1721, most of these people had left the area. Very few Europeans settled there for the next forty years.

In 1803, the United States bought the Louisiana region from France for $15 million. The land that is now Arkansas was included in the Louisiana Purchase. In the years that followed, thousands of settlers moved into the Arkansas region. Some arrived in covered wagons, while others rode flatboats down the Mississippi River. They built log cabins and planted vegetables and fruit trees. Many settlers farmed in central Arkansas and the northern hills. Others started growing cotton and tobacco in the rich **bottomlands** of the southeast. Many slaves were brought into Arkansas to work the cotton plantations along the Mississippi River. Slavery was legal in the southern states until the end of the American Civil War in 1865.

The early African Americans living in Arkansas did much for the new state. They constructed roads and homesteads, tended livestock, and harvested cotton.

Traditional plantation houses had long columns that supported an extended roof. This type of roof kept the house cool by keeping the sun away from the walls.

While most early settlers lived on farms and plantations, new towns began to form as well. Hot Springs was founded in 1807. This town was named for the hot springs that bubbled from the ground. In 1820, Little Rock was founded. It was situated by a **bluff**, which the French called *petit roche*, or "little rock."

The town of Fort Smith began as a United States army post in 1817. Arkansas became a territory in 1819, and Little Rock became the capital two years later. But Arkansas could not become a state at this time because its population was not large enough. In 1836, the population reached 60,000 people—the number required for statehood. In 1836, Arkansas became the twenty-fifth state in the United States.

QUICK FACTS

Arkansas's early pioneers enjoyed sports such as horse racing and bear hunting.

In 1835, Davy Crockett passed through Arkansas on his way to Texas. He spoke at a dinner given in his honor in Little Rock.

Sam Houston and his friends planned the 1836 Texas Revolution at the Old Tavern in Washington, Arkansas.

Although it was founded in 1812, Little Rock was not incorporated as a city until 1836.

On average, there are 49 people per square mile in Arkansas.

POPULATION

With more than 2.5 million people, Arkansas is the thirty-third largest state in population. Arkansas has always been an agricultural state, with a great number of people living in **rural** areas. About half the population lives on farms or in small towns. Most of the cities in Arkansas are small. Only twenty-nine of them have populations over 10,000.

Little Rock is the largest city in Arkansas, with a population of about 190,000. As the state capital, Little Rock is a center for government, education, transportation, and culture. Little Rock also has a "twin city," which lies across the Arkansas River—North Little Rock. This city has a population of about 65,000. Other large cities in the state include Fort Smith, Pine Bluff, Fayetteville, and Hot Springs.

QUICK FACTS

Arkansas is divided into seventy-five counties.

Arkansas's largest religious group is Baptist. In fact, there are about 1,400 Baptist congregations in the state.

The city of Texarkana lies on the Texas-Arkansas border. Texarkana, Texas, has about 32,000 people, while Texarkana, Arkansas, has about 23,000.

Every Memorial Day weekend, residents of Arkansas come together to enjoy Riverfest, the largest festival in the state.

Bill Clinton has played the saxophone since high school.

POLITICS AND GOVERNMENT

Many laws and important decisions are made in Little Rock. The state government is composed of three branches. The executive branch sets budgets and approves laws, and the legislative branch introduces new laws and changes existing ones. The judicial branch is comprised of the state courts.

The state legislature, or general assembly, consists of the Senate and the House of Representatives. The Senate has 35 members, while the House of Representatives has 100. On the federal level, there are two senators and four representatives that represent Arkansas in Washington, D.C.

Bill Clinton is a well-known political figure from Arkansas. He was elected governor of Arkansas in 1978, and served the state in this role for many years. Clinton then served as the president of the United States from 1993 to 2001. He was the nation's forty-second president.

QUICK FACTS

Bill Clinton was the youngest person ever to be elected governor of Arkansas. He was the third-youngest president of the United States.

James S. Conway was the first governor of the state of Arkansas.

The Capitol was built from 1899 to 1915. It sits on a hilltop west of downtown Little Rock. The building has large columns and a grand staircase, all made of marble.

Orval E. Faubus was the first Arkansas governor to be elected to six terms in office. He governed from 1955 to 1967. Faubus opposed the **integration** of Little Rock's schools for many years, earning criticism throughout the nation.

The legislature first met in the Arkansas State Capitol in 1911.

CULTURAL GROUPS

Ozark folk bands perform music that blends English, Scottish, and Irish musical traditions.

About 80 percent of Arkansans are of European heritage. European settlers came to the state from Ireland, Germany, England, and many other countries. Some of these newcomers settled in the Ozark Mountains. They created a rich folk culture with their own arts, crafts, music, and dances. These people lived in remote areas and often had very little money. They were **resourceful** and made many things by hand instead of buying them. The Ozark Folk Center in Mountain View works to preserve the cultural traditions of this region. There, visitors can see craftspeople making candles, baskets, and quilts. Local musicians may be seen at the Ozark Folk Center playing folk songs on hand-crafted fiddles, banjos, and guitars.

At the Ozark Folk Center, visitors can learn about the traditions of the people from the Ozark Mountains.

QUICK FACTS

The square dance is Arkansas's official state folk dance.

St. Mary's Catholic Church is found on Mount Bethel in northwestern Arkansas. It has four church bells, a 120-foot tower, and twenty-nine stained glass windows.

The Arkansas State Fiddler's Contest is held every September at the Ozark Folk Center in Mountain View.

The Little Rock Nine bravely fought against segregation in schools. They were later awarded the Congressional Gold Medal of Honor.

QUICK FACTS

In the early 1900s, many Chinese businessmen started grocery stores, laundries, and restaurants in communities across Arkansas.

Juneteenth is celebrated in many cities across Arkansas. On this day, African Americans mark the end of slavery in the southern states.

During World War II, Japanese Americans were placed in camps throughout the United States. Two of these camps were in Arkansas: Jerome and Rowher.

African Americans make up another important cultural group in Arkansas. When the first Africans were brought to Arkansas in the late 1700s, most of them worked as slaves on farms and plantations. Today, after many social reforms in the United States, African Americans participate in every area of society. Every February, Arkansas celebrates Black History Month. This is a time for African Americans to share and preserve their history and culture. Many people reflect on African Americans' long struggle for civil rights in the United States. In Little Rock, the Central High Museum and Visitor's Center honors the first African-American students who fought against **segregation** in schools.

At the time of European settlement, many groups of Native Peoples lived in the Arkansas area. Still, from 1820 to 1840 many Native Americans were forced to move to Oklahoma; this resulted in a decline of Arkansas's Native American population. Today, Native Americans account for only a small number of the state's residents. In total, there are about 14,000 Native Peoples living in Arkansas.

In Pine Bluff, there are several murals painted on buildings that depict the city's history and culture.

Before he started writing legal thrillers, John Grisham worked as a lawyer.

QUICK FACTS

The fiddle is Arkansas's state instrument.

WOK in Pine Bluff was Arkansas's first radio station. It began broadcasting in 1921.

Television station KATV in Little Rock began broadcasting in 1953.

Arkansas's first newspaper was the *Arkansas Gazette*. It was founded by William E. Woodruff at Arkansas Post in 1819.

ARTS AND ENTERTAINMENT

There is a thriving arts scene in Arkansas. Many people in the state use art, music, and the written word to share their ideas and experiences with others.

Some nationally acclaimed writers come from Arkansas. John Grisham writes legal thrillers. He has written many novels, including *The Firm*, *The Pelican Brief*, and *The Client*. Many of Grisham's novels have been made into successful movies.

Maya Angelou is considered one of the greatest voices in literature today. Angelou is a remarkable woman—she is a poet, novelist, actress, educator, and civil-rights activist. Angelou, who grew up in Stamps, has written eleven best-selling novels as well as poetry. She is best known for her book *I Know Why the Caged Bird Sings*. This book, published in 1970, tells of her childhood experiences in Arkansas.

In 1971, Maya Angelou became the first African-American woman to have an original screenplay produced.

Johnny Cash has recorded more than 500 albums and 1,500 songs.

Country music is a prominent part of Arkansas's arts and entertainment scene. Many well-known country singers come from the state. Johnny Cash was born near Kingsland and later moved to Dyess where his family farmed cotton. His daughter, Roseanne, is also a popular country singer. Glen Campbell is a native of Delight. He has had many hit records and was the host of his own variety show. Glen Campbell was even a member of the Beach Boys for a brief period.

The late Conway Twitty is yet another highly-acclaimed singer from Arkansas. Known as the "High Priest of Country Music," Twitty was born and raised in Helena, where he was known as Harold Jenkins. His stage name combines the names of two towns: Conway, Arkansas and Twitty, Texas.

Arkansas offers numerous cultural attractions for audiences. Little Rock is home to many of the state's theaters, museums, and musical venues. The Arkansas Symphony, the Decorative Arts Museum, and the Arkansas Arts Center are all based in Little Rock.

QUICK FACTS

Arkansas has an official state **anthem.** It is "Arkansas" by Eva Ware Barnett.

Actors Frank Bonner, Mary Steenburgen, and Jerry Van Dyke are all from Arkansas.

Little Rock Zoo is home to more than 600 native and exotic animals.

The Ozark Folk Center is just one of many attractions in Arkansas that celebrate and preserve the state's folk culture.

There are nearly 2,000 documented caves in northern Arkansas. Eight of them are open to the public.

SPORTS

With its mountains, streams, and beautiful scenery, the Natural State is the perfect place for outdoor sports and activities. Arkansas has more than 200 government-run campgrounds and many more private ones. There are countless day hikes, mountain bike paths, and **equestrian** trails to enjoy. People can even explore underground caves. Serious hikers can take an extended backpacking trip on the Ozark Highlands National Recreation Trail.

Bikers will enjoy touring through the mountains and valleys of northern Arkansas. This region has some of the most scenic and physically challenging bike tours in the United States. Bikers can also explore bike routes in the Mississippi Valley. They will find both hills and level stretches in this area.

Fishing and hunting are also popular pastimes in Arkansas. With more than 9,000 miles of streams, people can travel by canoe, **johnboat**, or raft. Known as a "fisher's haven," these waterways provide some of the world's best fishing. Bass, **walleye,** and many kinds of trout are found there.

QUICK FACTS

"Dizzy" and "Daffy" Dean came from Lucas, Arkansas, and went on to become major league pitchers. For many years the brothers pitched for the St. Louis Cardinals.

Arkansas is home to the World Championship Duck Calling Contest at Stuttgart.

Arkansas is a bass fisher's paradise. There are many varieties of bass in most of the lakes and rivers in the state.

QUICK FACTS

Little Rock's Brooks Robinson played third base for the Baltimore Orioles. He was elected to the Baseball Hall of Fame in 1982.

Scottie Pippen was a basketball star at Central Arkansas University. He later played for the Chicago Bulls and helped them become world champions in 1991, 1992, 1993, 1996, 1997, and 1998.

Lou Brock was born in El Dorado. He played baseball for the St. Louis Cardinals.

Many people take advantage of the golf courses found all over the state. In Arkansas, golfers can find courses in the mountains and on islands. There is even a golf course with its own marina. Because of the warm climate, golfers in Arkansas can enjoy teeing off all year round.

Many Arkansans enjoy watching and playing team sports. Football is especially popular in the state. The Razorbacks are the University of Arkansas's football team. They have won many post-season championships including the Orange Bowl, the Sugar Bowl, and the Cotton Bowl.

The Arkansas Razorbacks have two home stadiums. At the Razorback Stadium in Fayetteville and the War Memorial Stadium in Little Rock, the Razorbacks play in front of more than 50,000 fans.

Brain Teasers

1 How did Texarkana get its name?

Answer: The town of Texarkana lies on the border of Texas and Arkansas. It is also close to Louisiana. The name "Texarkana" is a combination of these three state names: TEXas, ARKansas, and LouisiANA.

2 Is there a rock in Little Rock?

Answer: Yes. Little Rock was named for an outcropping of rock along the Arkansas River. It was discovered by French explorer Jean Baptiste Bénard de La Harpe in 1722 and served as a landmark for people traveling along the river.

3 Mountain View, known for its authentic mountain music, is the world's largest maker of what instrument?

Answer: Mountain View is the largest producer of handmade dulcimers in the world. A dulcimer is a stringed instrument that lies on the player's lap. Sounds are produced by striking the strings with hammers.

4 What are Evening Shade, Okay, Toad Suck, Tomato, and Strawberry?

Answer: They are all towns in Arkansas.

5

Why are the people of Helena so "blue"?

Answer: Actually, the people are not blue, but their music is. The town is a hub of blues music in the state. An accomplished blues musician, Sonny Boy Williamson, made Helena his home for many years. The town hosts the King Biscuit Blues Festival each year.

6

Who were the "Little Rock Nine"?

Answer: In 1957, when schools in Little Rock began to integrate African American students into public schools, nine African-American students were blocked when they tried to enter Little Rock's Central High School. After three weeks of tension, President Eisenhower sent the 101st Airborne Division to protect the new students. The story of these nine brave students is preserved at the Central High Museum and Visitor's Center in Little Rock.

7

What is a "fried pie"?

Answer: A fried pie is a kind of pastry made in Arkansas. It consists of dried apples and peaches fried inside a golden pastry crust. Fried pies are a favorite of former president Bill Clinton.

8

What interesting artifacts can be found at Arkansas's Hampson Museum?

Answer: The Hampson Museum houses a large collection of artifacts left by the Nodena. The Nodena were farmers who lived during the Late Mississippi period, about 500 years ago. The collection was preserved by Dr. James K. Hampson and donated to the state in the 1950s.

FOR MORE INFORMATION

Books

Aylesworth, Thomas G. *South Central: Arkansas, Kansas, Louisiana, Missouri, Oklahoma*. New York: Chelsea House Publishers, 1996.

Fradin, Dennis B. *Arkansas*. Chicago: Children's Press, 1994.

National Geographic Society. *Our Fifty States.* Washington: National Geographic Society, 1978.

Web sites

You can also go online and have a look at the following Web sites:

Arkansas Parks and Tourism
http://www.arkansas.com

Arkansas Secretary of State
http://www.sosweb.state.ar.us

The Department of Arkansas Heritage
http://www.arkansasheritage.com

Official State of Arkansas Web Site
http://www.state.ar.us

The Ozark Folk Center
http://www.ozarkfolkcenter.com

Some Web sites stay current longer than others. To find other Arkansas Web sites, enter search terms, such as "Arkansas," "Bill Clinton," "Little Rock," or any other topic you want to research.

GLOSSARY

anthem: a song that celebrates a country or a state

archeologists: scientists who study early peoples through artifacts and remains

bayou: a marshy arm of a lake or river

bluff: a cliff or steep riverbank

bottomlands: low-lying lands around a waterway

endangered: a threatened species

equestrian: involving horses or horseback riding

expedition: a journey of exploration

integration: to bring people of different races together

johnboat: a narrow, flat-bottomed boat used on rivers and streams

plantations: estates where specific crops are grown, and sometimes tended by resident workers

refuges: places of shelter and protection

relocate: forcing a group of people to move to another location

resourceful: able to invent new ways to do or make things in difficult situations

rural: living in the country or on farms

segregation: forcing separation and restrictions based on race

vocational: a school that offers instruction in an occupation or trade

walleye: a kind of freshwater fish

INDEX